The oldest English reel extant, c.1720 (Piscatorial Society Collection), a Victorian gaff and the wicker creel owned by G. E. M. Skues, the great English fly fisherman. From the exhibition 'Going Fishing Then and Now' at Salisbury and South Wiltshire Museum in 1989.

OLD FISHING TACKLE

Nigel Dowden

Shire Publications Ltd

CONTENTS

Published in 1999 by Shire Publications Ltd, Cromwell House, Church Street, Princes Risborough, Buckinghamshire HP27 9AA, UK. (Website: www.shirebooks.co.uk)

Printed in Great Britain by CIT Printing Services Ltd, Press Buildings, Merlins Bridge, Haverfordwest, Pembrokeshire SA61 1XF.

British Library Cataloguing in Publication Data. A catalogue record for this book is available from the British Library.

ACKNOWLEDGEMENTS
Assistance in research was kindly given by Farlow's of Pall Mall; Michael Laycock, House of Hardy, Alnwick; Barry Meade, Forge Mill Needle Museum, Redditch; Guy Robinson, the Leckford Estate; Shakespeare Company (UK) Ltd; and Mrs Renee Wilson, Salisbury Museum. Other than the picture on the title page, which is from Salisbury Museum, and that on page 11, from the House of Hardy, all the tackle is from the author's collection or from old angling periodicals and catalogues. The photographs are all by Christel clear Photography.

Cover: A whole-cane and split-cane pole with a walnut Nottingham starback reel; a bait kettle; a Georgian cow-horn bait carrier; a French wicker creel; a Victorian leather fly wallet; a Hardy Birmingham-type trout fly reel c.1896; a C. C. de France split-cane trout fly rod from Hardy Bros, 1933; and a landing net with a cane handle.

A selection of Hardy trout fly reels dating from 1896.

Left: *An angler with rod, line, float and a barrel of fish from Dame Juliana Berners's 'Treatise of Fysshynge with an Angle', 1496.*

Right: *Detail of a tomb painting of c.2000 BC discovered in the Nile valley by Percy Newberry in 1893.*

THE FISHING ROD

Fishing with a rod and line was first illustrated in Britain in the fifteenth-century *Boke of St Albans* when Dame Juliana Berners completed her 'Treatise of Fysshynge with an Angle' in 1496. Four hundred years later the Egyptologist Percy Newberry discovered a picture of an angler with a similar rod, line and fish (*c.*2000 BC) on the wall of a tomb in the Nile valley. There is evidence of angling in China as long ago as 3000 BC.

In the most famous book on the subject, *The Compleat Angler* (1653), Izaak Walton explained what angling meant to him as a sport and pastime. In his conference with the hunter and the falconer he describes angling as 'my recreation, calm and quiet' and goes on to describe in some detail the tackle he used in the pursuit of various species of fish.

His equipment was very similar to that of the Egyptian angler. Both used a tapered rod of wood or reed with a line connected to the tip and a baited hook at the end of that line. Indeed, there was to be little development until the end of the eighteenth century when changes in tech-

nology and production were made possible by the industrial revolution.

From 1837, when Queen Victoria ascended the throne, until the 1930s the angler was at his most inventive and the British tackle industry at its most productive.

The production records kept by the major manufacturers are far from complete so it is fortunate for angling historians that there was great competition between them. Many manufacturers issued extensive annual catalogues of their products for both retailers and consumers. The catalogues which have survived, together with angling periodicals and books, provide much of the information available for researchers.

Since 1939 little has changed except for the raw materials used: plastic, nylon and carbon fibre have replaced cork, silk and wood in the angler's dictionary.

The simplest fishing rods were made from a single length of tapering material such as reed or wood. These had a natural springiness which assisted the angler in two ways. First, the rod was used to cata-

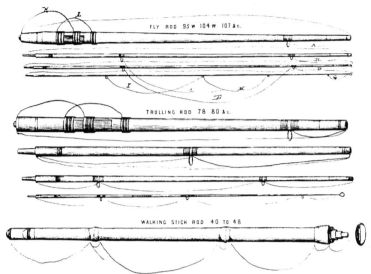

Three fishing rods illustrated in the Allcock catalogue of 1882: (top) a fly rod for trout fishing; (centre) a trolling rod (for fishing with a running line) for predatory fish such as pike; (bottom) a walking-stick rod hollowed to store the top sections of the rod.

pult or cast the baited line to the prey and then, when a fish was on the line, it would act as a shock absorber. The length of the rod depended on the materials available and on the size of the waters to be fished. By Walton's time rods of 7 yards (6.4 metres) and above were common. They were made up of six or more tapering sections, whipped together with fine thread. Pine was used for the butt, and pliable woods such as hazel and willow for the tip. At the end of every season the rod would be taken apart, each section oiled and the pieces stored in a dry place for the winter so that they would not distort.

The inconvenience of wandering the countryside with a 20 foot (6 metre) fishing pole was eventually overcome, first with simple jointed sockets between the sections and later with the perfection of the metal ferrule, which enabled a rod to be assembled and dismantled at will. But spliced rods continued to be made well into the twentieth century, because some anglers believed that they performed better than those with metal ferrules.

Izaak Walton's seventeenth-century rod was complex and multi-sectioned but it was still nothing more than a pole with a tight line. The line was attached to the tip of the rod and his casting range was therefore limited. Anglers first overcame this shortcoming by using a longer line, which would lie in a coil on the ground in front of them and which could be cast on to the water through a ring at the tip of the pole. This cumbersome practice was eliminated by adding extra rings to the pole and attaching to it a reel or winch which stored the loose line.

In the nineteenth century imported bamboo from the Far East and greenheart and lancewood from South America were used to improve rod construction. The South American hardwoods were particularly strong and pliable, while bamboo was cheap, easy to work and quickly spliced into a tapering length. Whalebone was often used for rod tips.

Heavy solid wood and whole-cane rods continued to be made well into the twentieth century despite the appearance, in the second half of the nineteenth, of rods built of split bamboo cane. At first the process was used to construct just the flexible tip section for a greenheart or whole-cane rod but eventually the entire lightweight rod was constructed of split cane. It was made up of six pieces of cane sliced

4

Hardy's 'Lock Fast' ferrule patented in 1897. The lug on the top section engaged the thread on the lower section.

Two Farlow rods: (top) a three-piece spliced cane 'Denham' salmon rod c.1939, and (below) a trout fly rod with metal ferrules made for Farlow by the French company Pezon & Michel c.1964.

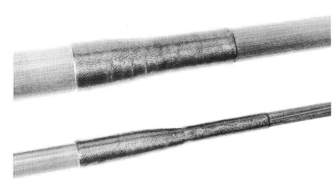

Spliced whole-cane joints on an Allcock 13 foot (3.9 metre) 'Peerless' match rod made in the 1950s and used for coarse fishing. The top joint is whipped whole cane and the lower joint is whole cane to the split-cane tip.

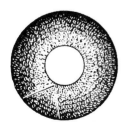 

A series of diagrams from Allcock's catalogue of 1912 showing the steps in building a split-cane rod: (left to right) Cane from which sections are cut; sections ready for cementing; sections cemented; sections with steel centre.

from the whole bamboo shoot, each of which was accurately planed to a triangular section. The pieces were then glued and whipped together, sometimes around a steel core, to form a strong and flexible stick.

Credit for the invention of the split-cane method is disputed but it is clear that development was taking place on both sides of the Atlantic in the mid nineteenth century.

In 1872 the firm of Hardy Bros was started in Alnwick, Northumberland, originally to produce cutlery, but the two brothers soon turned their engineering skills to the manufacture of guns and fishing tackle. Their reputation as tackle makers grew rapidly and they showed a wide range of products at the London Fisheries Exhibition in March 1894. J. W. Blakey, writing in the magazine *Northern Angler*, wrote of Hardy's exhibit: 'I could scarcely tear myself away from amongst the split cane trout rods and admired a great many, from a little ten foot rod weighing five-and-a-half ounces to the powerful dry fly patterns.' Blakey particularly liked Har-

dy's 'Perfection' trout rod, which he described as 'a clinking good rod at something like £3 3s'. The Perfection was one of more than one hundred different types of cane rod built by Hardy Bros from 1872 and it continued in production until the 1960s.

Hardy Bros were among the best of many firms producing split-cane rods in Britain. They often named particular models after well-known rivers such as the Itchen, Kennet and Wye, and lakes like Loch Lomond and Loch Leven. Even famous anglers and writers of their day such as John Bickerdyke, angling editor of *The Field*, lent their names to Hardy rods. While Hardy Bros were establishing their reputation in Europe, similar developments were taking place in the United States of America, particularly in New England.

The Shakespeare and Orvis factories were producing good-quality split-cane rods in quantity by the end of the nineteenth century but by far the finest rods were produced by Hiram Lewis Leonard of Maine. One of the greatest fly fishermen and writers of his time was a London solicitor, G. E. M. Skues. He fished the river Itchen in Hampshire between 1883 and 1938 with an 8 foot (2.4 metre) split-cane trout rod built by Leonard and he was so pleased with its action that he dubbed it 'WBR' – the World's Best Rod.

By the end of the nineteenth century it was possible to buy a rod for every possible angling challenge. Short and stocky rods, 6 or 7 feet (1.8 to 2.1 metres) in length, were favoured by sea anglers who fished from boats. There was no need for them to cast their bait since they fished from above the prey. Their rods needed to be short, for convenience on the boat, and strong to carry a heavy weight in tidal waters. Greenheart was a much favoured wood for boat-fishing rods because of its natural resistance to salt water.

Beach fishermen demanded a very different type of rod. They had to cast a weight a considerable distance from the

The Hardy Bros stall at the 1894 Crystal Palace Exhibition.

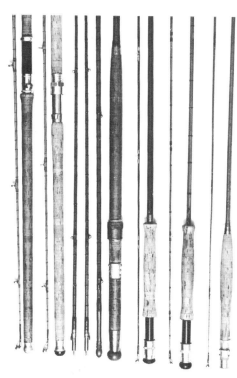

Some of the author's Hardy rods: (left to right) spinning rod (1946), LRH No. 1 spinning rod (1958), Wye salmon rod (1931), 'Invincible' fly rod (1967), 'Perfection' fly rod (1960), C. C. de France fly rod (1933).

their bait into the swim where a chub or a perch might lie. They had no need to cast their bait any great distance and they kept the gap between rod tip, float and water at a minimum to enable a quick strike when the fish took.

Trout and salmon fishermen have always kept their bait on the move by casting and recasting their flies over the water. The weight of the fishing line itself, not a lead weight, carried the gut cast and fly to the fish. Line was stripped from the reel and kept in the air as the fisherman flicked the rod backwards and forwards in a series of false casts. When enough line had been paid out, the fly was allowed to drop gently on the water on the final forward cast. Fly rods were made to be very pliable, not just to cope with the constant flexing during casting but also to absorb the severe shocks that could be

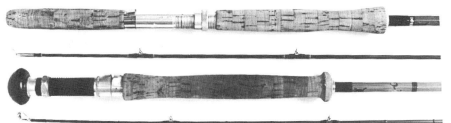

Two 'The Scottie' split-cane trout rods made by Sharpe of Aberdeen in about 1950, one showing the extension handle attached below the reel seat for two-handed casting.

shore in order to get their bait to the fish. This required a long and flexible rod which reached perfection with the arrival of the split-cane method of construction.

Freshwater rods were developed to cater both for those who fished for game fish, such as salmon and trout, and those who fished for coarse fish. The term 'coarse' refers to all species of freshwater fish other than those of the salmon family. Coarse fishermen favoured rods which were long (up to 30 feet, 9 metres) and stiff and which enabled them to swing

delivered by a fighting trout or salmon. Rods made for trout fishing were normally used single-handed and ranged from 7 feet long (2.1 metres) for fishing on a small brook up to 11 feet (3.4 metres) for a fast-flowing southern chalk stream. Salmon rods were longer, from 13 to 16 feet (4.0 to 4.9 metres), and much sturdier to cope with the size of the prey. They were used two-handed.

Spinning rods bridged the gap between sea and freshwater fishing. Spinning became the term used to describe a method

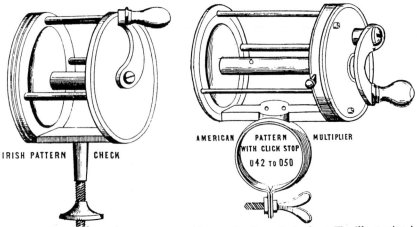

IRISH PATTERN   CHECK

AMERICAN   PATTERN   MULTIPLIER
WITH CLICK STOP
042 TO 050

Left: *This early winch was secured to the rod by a spike through the butt. The illustration is from Allcock's catalogue of 1866.*
Right: *A winch with a collar rod fitting shown in the 1866 Allcock's catalogue.*

of fishing for predatory fish with an artificial bait which, when drawn through the water, spun or wobbled in such a way that it resembled the fish's natural food. A spinning rod would be between 8 and 10 feet (2.4 and 3.0 metres) long and flexible enough to cast the lure a long distance, while having enough strength to withstand the aggressive take of a predatory game fish. Bass and sea trout in the estuaries and salmon or pike in fresh water were often fished on spinning rods with artificial lures.

While the rod was developing, the use of the reel was becoming widely accepted as the best method of storing line while fishing. In the early days the reel was attached to the rod by means of a spike

through the butt, while later reels had a collar which clamped around it. Both of these finally gave way to the reel seat, which enabled the reel to be attached and removed from the butt with the minimum of effort. Early reel seats consisted of little more than two sliding rings which were pressed over the reel foot, a method which is still in use today for its simplicity and light weight. By the beginning of the twentieth century a number of screw-threaded reel seats had been patented which gave greater security and virtually eliminated the accidental loss of the reel.

The line passed from the reel through the rod tip via a series of rings whipped on at intervals along the length of the rod. Many types of ring were designed to coun-

Two sliding rings secure this reel to a match rod. This Allcock rod was made in the mid 1950s but the method of reel attachment dates back to the nineteenth century. It remains popular because it is simple and light.

8

Hardy's 'Universal' reel fitting with a secure slot and a sliding ring on this 1933 trout fly rod.

This Hardy salmon rod of 1931 showed a further advance in development of the reel seat with a secure slot and a screw ring.

Left: *Screw reel seat on a 1961 Hardy 'Perfection' trout fly rod.*

Below: *A Hardy spinning-rod reel seat of 1946. The foot of the reel was placed between the two sliding rings and the hexagonal nut tightened securely with a small spanner supplied with the rod. Spinning rods were used to cast and retrieve light artificial lures when fishing for predatory fish such as pike or bass.*

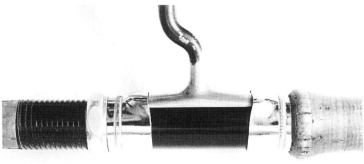

Wire snake ring on a 1933 split-cane trout fly rod. These simple rings were all that was needed to guide a weighted fly line from the reel during the cast.

Bridge snake ring on a 1931 split-cane salmon rod. The bridge helped keep the line from abrading against the varnished cane during casting.

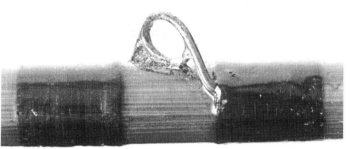

'Bell's Life' stand-off ring on a 1950 whole-cane match rod. Match fishermen used lines as light as 2 pounds (0.9 kg) breaking strain, which could stick to the rod when wet. The stand-off ring kept the line away from the rod.

The tip ring, lined with agate, on a 1946 spinning rod. Agate was used to resist the abrasiveness of the line.

Agate-lined stand-off tip ring on a 1950 coarse fishing rod.

Butt ring to a 1946 Hardy spinning rod. Note that the lower whipping is of copper wire, and not silk, to add strength.

teract the problem of friction as the line rubbed against the rings and the rod. For the fly fisher, the snake wire ring proved to be the favourite while coarse anglers found the stand-off 'Bell's Life' intermediate ring ideal for their light lines. Agate or porcelain was often used to line the tip and butt rings of rods, since these two spots incurred the greatest wear from lines which were made of silk or twine and which abraded bare nickel rings.

Rod building eventually became a precise engineering process, enabling manufacturers to build rods to exacting specifications. By attaching a weight to the tip, the maker would bend the prototype rod in a controlled manner. The shape and amount of the curve provided the information that enabled him accurately to calculate the optimum strength of line and the optimum weight needed to cast the line effectively. Test curves also enabled him to provide his customer with the rod best suited to the waters he fished and with precise details of the most appropriate tackle. The major manufacturers were turning out hundreds of rods each week at the beginning of the twentieth century and, although this might be imagined as mass production, much of the skilled construction was done by hand.

L. R. Hardy examines a trout fly rod in the factory stores at the Alnwick factory in 1950. With him are Fred Hardy, wearing glasses, and Bill Blackburn, the factory manager. Quality control was paramount at Hardy Bros and their reputation was jealously guarded.

A 3¹/₂ inch (89 mm) all-brass winch (left) with a curved crank handle and a wooden knob, c.1840; (right) a 2¹/₄ inch (57 mm) all-brass winch with crank handle recessed into an anti-foul rim.

THE FISHING REEL

The first fishing reels, or 'wynches' as they were then known, appeared in Britain in the seventeenth century. The earliest known examples were of simple wooden construction with end plates separated by a number of pillars and, between the plates, a spool which revolved on the centrally located spindle. The spool was turned by a crank handle. Few have survived but a number of eighteenth-century Scottish reels, known as 'pirns', exist which are similar in construction.

By the beginning of the nineteenth century there were a number of manufacturers producing durable winches made of brass, among them a London manufacturer called Ustonson who is known to have supplied George IV. Brass was an ideal material for fishing reels since it was not subject to corrosion or distortion when exposed to water. There was little change in the basic design of reels until the middle of the nineteenth century, and spiked and collared winches with simple crank-wind drums between two plates were still being offered by Allcock in 1866.

Crank-wind reels were operated by means of a handle fixed to the drum at its central point. As the reel became more widely accepted as a means of storing line a major drawback became apparent: it was easy for the line to become wrapped around the handle when playing a fish. This was first overcome with the introduction of anti-foul rims. The crank handle was recessed into a raised rim on the plate, thereby closing the gap through which stray line might pass and become wrapped around the central spindle.

The crank wind was to become virtually obsolete with the introduction in the second half of the nineteenth century of

Three Nottingham reels (c.1890-1910) developed for and by river Trent anglers. (Left to right): 3¹/₂ inch (89 mm) starback reel with optional check, brass centrepiece and bone handles; 4 inch (102 mm) straight-back reel with optional check and ebonite handles; 3¹/₂ inch (89 mm) starback reel with optional check, ebonite handles and Slater drum latch which enabled the drum to be detached from the backplate.

Two Nottingham reels showing brass fittings on the backplates. These are described as straight-back and starback reels. Both have buttons to engage an optional check.

The check mechanism inside a Nottingham reel. The triangular pin, or pawl, was moved by the button on the backplate and was held in place by the circular spring. When the check was applied the pin would engage with a cog on the spool and prevent it from running freely.

A 3 inch (76 mm) starback Nottingham reel made by Sowerbutts of London for freshwater fishing in about 1920. The button on the brass strap operates the optional check.

Above right: *A 4½ inch (114 mm) starback Nottingham reel made by Carter & Company of London for sea fishing in about 1900. Apart from an optional check mechanism, this reel has a wing nut which not only secures the drum to the backplate but can also be used to exert pressure or drag when fishing. Note, too, the brass line guide invented by John Bickerdyke, a well-known angler who was once angling editor of 'The Field'.*

reels where the handle was attached to the drum at the outer edge of the plate rather than at the centre, thereby eliminating the crank altogether. Allcock's catalogue of 1866 shows such a reel and refers to it as a rotary winch. Factories in the Midlands were producing large numbers of plate-wind reels by the late nineteenth century and they were often sold through retailers who stamped them with their own individual mark. They are often referred to as Birmingham reels.

In another part of the Midlands a type of reel was being developed for and by anglers who fished the river Trent. This was no more than a wooden drum which

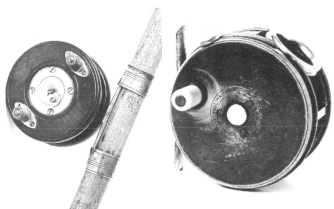

Far left: *A 3 inch (76 mm) starback Nottingham reel made by Sowerbutts for freshwater fishing in about 1920. The button in the centre operates a spring-loaded catch to release the drum from the reel. Its invention is credited to the Nottinghamshire tackle maker David Slater of Newark.*

Left: *A 3½ inch (89 mm) Hardy 'Perfect' trout fly reel made in 1917 of aluminium with a brass drum.*

revolved around a spindle located at the centre of a single plate. Such reels became known as Nottingham reels and their construction lasted well into the twentieth century. The first Nottingham reels had the disadvantage that, even when varnished, they would swell and distort when wet and this made casting and rewinding difficult. A straight, or sometimes a star-shaped, brass strap was often fitted to the backplate in order to minimise the risk of distortion, but Nottingham reels became truly free-running only when wooden drums were replaced with brass ones.

Control of the line during the cast and retrieve also caused problems with free-running centre-pin reels, and ratchet mechanisms were introduced to check the speed at which the drum could spin. Checks were either fixed or optionally engaged by means of a button on the backplate. Another method of control was achieved by use of a spring and wing nut on the centre-pin which enabled the pressure or drag on the drum to be varied.

The most famous Nottinghamshire manufacturer of centre-pin reels was David Slater of Newark. A coachbuilder by trade, he began making rods in 1852 and, later, wooden and ebonite reels. He is credited with inventing the 'Slater latch', a small spring-loaded catch which enabled the drum to be removed from the reel in an instant. There is no evidence that he registered a patent for the design and it was copied by reel makers all over Britain.

The two most famous centre-pin reels of all time were introduced in the last decade of the nineteenth century by Hardy Bros, who announced the 'Perfect' fly reel, while Allcock of Redditch took on the development of Henry Coxon's 'Aerial' reel.

The first Hardy 'Perfect' reel appeared in the company's catalogue in 1891 and they claimed that it had taken three years to develop. The Birmingham 'Half Ebonite' and 'Hercules' reels were already in many retailer's catalogues but this new centre-pin reel was unique in that the drum ran on ball-bearings, making it virtually friction-free. The Hardy 'Perfect' was

This illustration of Coxon's 'Aerial' reel (Model 4104 in the Allcock range of tackle) appeared in 1901.

Two nineteenth-century salmon reels sold by Hardy Bros: (left) the oval Hardy logo dates the 4 inch (102 mm) brass and ebonite Birmingham reel to c.1890; (right) a 4¹/₂ inch (114 mm) bronze 'Hercules' reel, bearing the famous Hardy 'rod in hand' logo used before 1890, made of a special alloy which Hardy Bros claimed was up to one-third lighter than brass.

The interior of a Hardy 'Perfect' trout fly reel showing the ball-bearing race which made the drum virtually friction-free. The mechanism at the top of the picture enabled the tension of the check to be varied when playing a fish. This particular check was introduced in 1917.

originally made completely in brass and later in aluminium. More than 170 different variations have borne the name over the years.

Henry Coxon was a well-known angler and writer at the end of the nineteenth century and he is generally credited with the invention of the 'Aerial' reel. It was much lighter than other Nottingham reels available at the time because, as on a bicycle wheel, he used spokes to attach the hub of the drum to the flanges. Allcock of Redditch perfected the reel and commenced production in 1896. As well as being half the weight of the equivalent wooden reel, the skeletal construction and the (later) pierced flanges speeded up the drying of the line as it was retrieved from the water.

Allcock achieved near perfection in 1939 when they announced their 'Match Aerial' at £2 2s. This version of the reel incorporated all the usual 'Aerial' quality

Two Allcock 'Aerial' reels of the 1930s: (left) a 3³/4 inch (95 mm) perforated drum model made in aluminium with Bickerdyke line guide; (right) a 4 inch (102 mm) 'Aerial Popular' all-aluminium model.

but its drum was little more than half an inch (13 mm) wide, which made for rapid line recovery. The production run was short, curtailed by the start of the Second World War, and although a model was announced by the company in 1946 the post-war Aerial never came up to the same standard. Production continued until Allcock ceased trading in the 1960s.

Casting with a centre-pin reel called for some degree of skill and inventive Victorian anglers were always seeking ways of achieving greater distances. Reels such as the Scarborough type of sea-fishing reel had no check or brake, so the angler had to stop the reel spinning as soon as possible after the cast was complete. If he failed to apply a brake on the reel it would tend to spin on and continue to discharge line for some time after the weight had come to a rest. The result more often than not was the familiar bird's nest of tangled line.

In May 1878 a Mr G. R. Holding applied for a patent which was to revolutionise angling. He took an ordinary Nottingham centre-pin reel and mounted on a small turntable which was secured in the reel seat. The drum of the reel could be turned at 90 degrees to the rod so that when the weight was cast forward the line spilled over the side of the reel while the spool remained stationary. When the cast was complete the drum was returned to the conventional position and the line was retrieved normally.

The next major step toward the fixed-spool reel came from the Scottish angler P. D. Malloch, who in 1884 patented his sidecasting or spinning reel. This reel also

Four bakelite centre-pin reels made in the 1930s: (left to right) a 3 inch (76 mm) Allcock 'Aerialite' trout reel; a 3¼ inch (83 mm) 'Gyrex' centre-pin reel with line guide, optional check and variable drag; a 3¼ inch (83 mm) 'Modernite' centre pin reel with brass straightback, optional check and variable drag; a 3¼ inch (83 mm) Allcock 'Aerialite' centre-pin reel with optional check.

Left: *A 5 inch (127 mm) 'Aerialite' sea-fishing reel in black bakelite. Allcock claimed that it could not warp or corrode nor was it affected by extremes of temperature. In 1934 this reel sold for 16 shillings.* Right: *The swivel winch in casting position.*

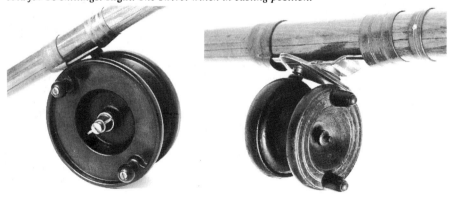

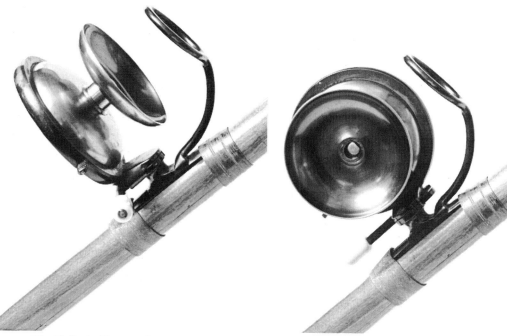

The Malloch sidecaster in casting position (left) and (right) in retrieve position.

had the facility to allow the drum to be turned at 90 degrees to the rod for the cast, but Malloch produced a convex drum which allowed the line to spill over the side more easily. While there are few examples of Holding's swivel winch, Malloch's sidecaster remained in production for more than fifty years and a number of modifications were made during its lifetime.

One major drawback of all the early sidecasting reels was that they caused the line to kink as it was cast and then retrieved, kinking it a little more each time. Malloch then made his sidecaster drum detachable and reversible and advised that it should be reversed after every other cast so that the kinks introduced by one cast would be eliminated by the next. This worked, but it meant that while the reel was rewound with a normal clockwise action after one cast, reversing the drum for the next cast also reversed the direction for the rewind. This cumbersome process was finally overcome by the introduction of the Erskine Malloch reel in 1932, which had a rather complex series of gears enabling the reel to be rewound clockwise at all times.

The true principle of the fixed spool was developed by A. H. Illingworth with his 1905 'Threadline' reel, so named because of its ability to cast a very fine line. Illingworth was a Yorkshire weaver and his idea came from the bobbins of thread used on looms in his mill. They did not rotate and the thread spilled from the bobbins over the edge. Illingworth's prototypes used the same principle. In this case the drum remained at 90 degrees to the rod at all times. The line was returned to the reel by means of a metal arm or flyer which rotated around the drum. While the fixed spool and the flyer were significant developments of the Holding and Malloch inventions, Illingworth made another most important discovery. When a fish took his bait he was unable to play the fish by giving it line unless he freed the line entirely by taking it from the flyer. This problem was overcome by his introduction of a friction clutch arrangement which

17

enabled the drum to rotate when a great strain was put on the line.

By 1920 Allcock had introduced the Allcock-Stanley light casting reel, which retailed for little more than £1 and was particularly recommended in their advertising for 'trout, pike and salmon spinning, whilst it is also excellent for swimming a worm or gentle for all coarse fish'. It sold in large numbers but it, too, had the disadvantage that it introduced kinks into the angler's line. Although Allcock provided booklets with the reel and included letters from satisfied customers, they withdrew it after fourteen years.

In 1932 Hardy Bros introduced their first two 'Altex' fixed-spool reels which, together with a later No. 3 model, remained in production for more than thirty years. In 1937 a cheaper model called the 'Hardex' was introduced but this was discontinued in 1959.

By that time fixed-spool reels had become the most popular type of reel for many types of angling. Apart from the simplicity of casting, its geared rewinding action meant that one turn of the handle resulted in multiple winds around the drum and therefore a faster retrieval of the line.

Multiplier reels were known to the Vic-

A Hardy 'Altex' No. 2 Mark V fixed-spool reel made from 1932 until 1959. The star on the front of the spool operated a clutch mechanism which allowed line to be stripped from the reel by a running fish while the reel continued to be wound in.

18

torian angler. There are examples of multiplier winches dating back to the eighteenth century and Ustonson supplied one to George IV in about 1800. Even so, this type of geared reel failed to achieve any significant popularity until almost one hundred years later, when high-quality models were developed in the United States.

The multiplier reel bore some similarities to the earliest wooden winches. The drum was contained between two plates and the rewind was by a crank handle.

The crank handle of the multiplier, however, was not directly attached to the drum but was set slightly off centre on the plate. Between the outer plate and the drum was a gearbox which transformed one turn of the handle into as many as four times the turn of the drum. The reel was used in both freshwater and sea fishing and was made in sizes from $1^{1}/_{2}$ inches to 6 inches (38-150 mm) and more in diameter.

Multiplier reels were designed to run freely during the cast. They were generally used on top of the rod rather than under it and during the cast the speed of the drum was regulated by the angler's thumb on the line. Casting with a multiplier was just as difficult as casting with a free-running centre-pin reel and the bird's nest tangle was a common problem. Automatic brakes and governors were added to some reels in an attempt to solve the problem, but practice was the only real answer.

Small multiplier reels were used by freshwater anglers to spin for trout, and larger versions for pike and salmon. Beach fishermen learned to achieve huge distances when casting with these free-running reels and the largest models became widely used in big-game fishing at sea.

Three American multiplier reels: (left to right) a $3^{1}/_{4}$ inch (83 mm) Four Bros Sumco reel number 2257 with three patent numbers from the 1920s, optional check; a $2^{1}/_{4}$ inch (57 mm) Shakespeare 'President' reel with line guide (invented in 1897) which moved along the reel as line was retrieved, laying it evenly on the drum; a $1^{3}/_{4}$ inch (44 mm) Atlas 'Portage' reel with separate check and drag controls.

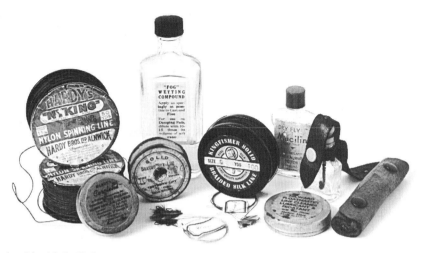

Spools of braided silk line from the 1950s, with dressings, hooks, gut and other equipment essential before synthetics replaced natural materials.

THE LINE, THE HOOK AND THE BAIT

The practice of twisting the hair from a horse's tail to construct a fishing line was used by the Greeks in the first century AD and horsehair lines were still in use in the nineteenth century. White hair was preferred by anglers since it was thought to be virtually invisible to the fish in clear water, but it could also be dyed to match the colour of weed. Anglers would often make their own lines with the aid of an engine or twisting machine. This ingenious device had three small cogs with a hook at each axis and these were made to rotate by a larger cog turned by a handle. The hairs were suspended from the hooks by a weight and as the handle was turned the three strands became twisted together. The angler would make up as many links as he required and would join them all together to finish the line. By varying the number of hairs used, the thickness, and therefore the strength, of the line could be controlled. Invisibility was of paramount importance and it was generally agreed that the line should taper so that the end section would consist of no more than two hairs. Izaak Walton described the selection, the twisting and the dyeing of horsehair lines in considerable detail. He advised the choice of hairs of equal thickness, 'for such do usually stretch all together, and break all together, which hairs of an unequal bigness never do, but break singly and so deceive the angler that trusts to them'. He then boiled the line in a dye based on strong ale, soot and the juice extracted from walnut-tree leaves.

By the end of the eighteenth century silk began to replace horsehair but, although stronger, it was substantially more expensive. For salmon fishing the angler

Two twisting machines illustrated in a late nineteenth-century catalogue by Allcock of Redditch.

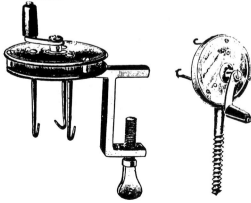

Corona silk fly lines made for salmon and trout fly fishing by Hardy Bros were of the highest quality and cost up to £3 for 42 yards (38 metres) in 1939.

Hardy 'Tournament' silk fly lines were very popular at about £1 each but were not so highly finished as the Corona.

was advised to have at least 100 yards (91 metres) of dressed silk eight-plait line, while for trout a finer line of dressed silk was considered best. Hair and silk mixtures were available but they were regarded as inferior. The dressings with which lines were made waterproof were numerous but a particularly easy method of dressing a line was by applying a solution of paraffin or cobbler's wax and spirits of wine to the line with a brush or feather. The wax remained after the spirit had evaporated.

For pike fishing Victorian anglers used end traces of gimp, which was silk whipped round with fine brass wire to add strength and to prevent it being cut by the fish's sharp teeth. The brass wire was dulled before use.

Because they were strong, and much cheaper than silk, by the end of the nineteenth century cotton lines were becoming popular for freshwater angling and flax lines for saltwater fishing.

At the end of the line a length of gut was attached. This was extracted from the silkworm caterpillar and treated and stretched until it was up to 20 inches (500 mm) in length. Gut casts were strong and were almost invisible to the fish in the water. The gut would also accept dye and steeping it in green tea or boiled onions was considered useful by some anglers. Ink, alum and even soot were also used.

The silk line and the gut cast were to remain in continuous use by anglers until well into the twentieth century. At the

A Hardy 'Compact' line drier introduced in 1937.

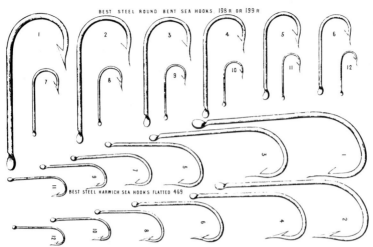

A variety of hooks from Allcock's catalogue of 1896, which also advertised sewing needles.

end of each day's fishing the line would be taken from the reel, thoroughly dried, either by draping it over the back of a chair or on a line drier, and then treated to prevent it from rotting. Used gut casts might be stored or discarded. In the mid 1930s nylon gut casts began to appear, often advertised as 'synthetical'. The production of monofilament nylon was eventually perfected to such a degree that entire fishing lines could be accurately constructed in continuous lengths, eventually replacing silk and cotton lines almost completely.

It is not surprising that fishing hooks and sewing needles were often made in the same factory. The most famous firm was that of the Allcock family of Redditch in Worcestershire, founded in 1803 by Polycarp Allcock. His son Samuel expanded the business until it became the largest manufacturer of fishing tackle in the world by the beginning of the twentieth century. Many other factories opened and eventually Redditch became the main centre for fishing-tackle manufacture in Britain.

The bait which the angler attached to the hook depended on the nature of his quarry. The simplest method, and one which is still practised, was to embed the hook in a morsel of food which the fish would recognise and eat. The maggot of the bluebottle, also called a gentle, has always been widely used as a live bait and this tiny grub is responsible for angling's description as 'the gentle art'. Worms, bread paste and even corn are other baits.

Coarse fishermen select a bait which attracts the prey by smell and then taste, while game fishermen use artificial lures in the form of spinners, plugs or flies.

Artificial baits have been used for centuries and Izaak Walton was a great exponent of fishing for trout with an artificial minnow when live bait was not available. He describes in great detail how he had an artificial minnow made for him by a seamstress who copied it from a live one. 'The mold or body of the Minnow was cloth, and wrought upon or over it thus with a needle', he said and went on: 'The back of it with very sad French green silk, and paler green silk towards the belly, shadowed as perfectly as you can imagine, just as you see a minnow'. He went on to describe the fins, the tail and the eyes and concluded: 'All of it so curiously wrought, and so exactly dissembled, that it would beguile any sharp-sighted trout in a swift stream'. Minnows have since been modelled in wood, rubber and metal to various designs. Real minnows, sprats and prawns, both alive and dead, were widely used for salmon

22

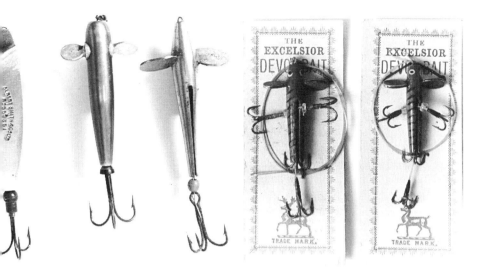

Above left: *Three Devon minnows used for salmon, trout and sea trout: (left to right) an aluminium Sunray 'Reflex' Devon from Albert Smith; an aluminium Milward's minnow with adjustable fins; a slotted brass minnow from Foster Bros.*

Above right: *The Excelsior slotted Devon bait from Allcock on original card mounts and dating from the 1920s. The smaller is only 1 inch (25 mm) long and they were tied to gut casts.*

Above: *Three artificial minnows from Hardy Bros which they called 'Sprat Devons' and made in silver or gold and other colours to special order from 1935.*

Right: *These artificial baits were in production in many factories between 1880 and 1930: (top) a 3 inch (76 mm) swallow-tail bait popular with pike fishermen; (bottom left) a quill minnow and (bottom right) a silk minnow, both used for trout.*

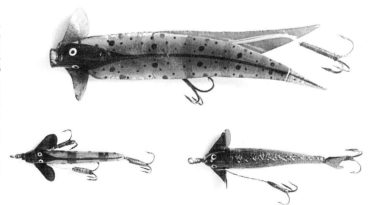

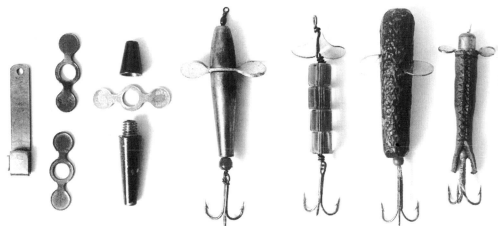

Left: *Rose-pattern minnows from about 1954. The fins of these aluminium lures were secured between the head and the tail. The small tool on the left was used to bend the fins to the desired angle, thus determining the speed at which the lure would spin during the retrieve.*
Right: *Three unusual old spinning lures in the author's collection: (left) a home-made minnow constructed with four amber beads; (centre) a hollow piece of stag horn, also home-made; and (right) a brass lure with a leather jacket sewn over, known as a leather eel tail – a popular bait for salmon and pike in Ireland.*

and pike as well as trout, and many ingenious rigs called 'flights' were constructed in order to present the bait and deceive the fish.

A simple spoon-shaped lure was found to be extremely successful for attracting plaice in estuaries, while a shiny fish-shaped spoon was deadly for mackerel and sea bass when retrieved through the water and made to oscillate to suggest the movement of a small fish.

One of the more exacting methods of deceiving fish is practised by trout and salmon fishermen, who developed numer-

Left: *Three Hardy spoons made from Sheffield plate. Each has a three- pronged hook called a treble, and the one on the right is attached to the spoon by a chain to resist the sharp teeth of an aggressive pike.*
Right: *These spinners were patented by P. Geen in 1910 but were marketed by Allcock. The blade of the lure revolved around a central spindle and treble hooks were attached in two places.*

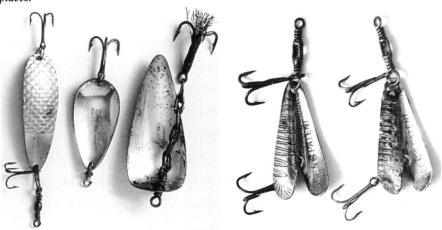

Left: *Pike fishing with plugs was very popular in the USA and this plug was patented in 1916. The fin close to the mouth of the lure made the plug dive in the water when it was retrieved by the angler. By varying the speed of the retrieve the plug would rise and dive like an injured fish, an easy prey for the pike. The pike would always attack with great speed and often go for the underside of the prey and the three trebles were placed to cover all directions of attack.*

The Serpentanic spinner was a flexible metal bait made exclusively by Bartleet.

A selection of artificial flies.

ous designs and patterns of flies using feather, silk and fur tied to a hook. The objective of the trout fisherman was to imitate the trout's natural food, either with a floating or dry fly or with a nymph, which is an imitation of the fly in its larval state and lives beneath the surface. The aim of the salmon fisherman was different. When the salmon returns from the sea to the river for breeding it stops feeding. It is generally agreed that the salmon reacts to the angler's fly out of annoyance rather than hunger and salmon fly tiers are still using patterns designed in the nineteenth century.

By the very nature of their use, there are few examples extant of early line, bait and hooks.

The firm of Wheatley was famous for its 'Silmalloy' fly boxes, made of aluminium with clips and, sometimes, chenille bars inside. This 1930s box had one compartment for flies and another for gut casts.

ACCESSORIES

The average angler had available to him an extensive range of accessories. Hooks, flies, bait and other items of tackle had to be stored in convenient receptacles; he needed tackle and clothing for wading in rivers and lakes, equipment for landing and storing the catch. Accessories featured prominently in the catalogues of the major tackle manufacturers of the nineteenth century.

Before the arrival of the hook with an eye, hooks were made with a flattened or spade end and this was usually supplied tied to a gut cast so that the angler had only to attach the cast to his line. Fly fishermen could buy their flies already tied to gut casts but in all cases the gut needed to be dampened before use to make it supple. Circular cast holders with sponge or felt dampers were very popular at the beginning of the twentieth century and continued to be made until the 1930s, when artificial gut or nylon casts became available. Allcock's catalogue of 1912 shows an aluminium cast box with a gray-

ling embossed on the lid, while by 1930 Hardy Bros had introduced an attractive bakelite model with a wire inlay and a motif of flies on the lid.

Storing bait was not difficult for the fly fisherman since his neatly prepared flies were safely kept in his fly reservoir and then transferred to a pocket fly container for the day. Likewise the angler spinning for pike or bass had little inconvenience in transporting his plugs and lures to the fishing ground. The bait angler, however, had a greater problem as he had to carry live minnows, worms or maggots. The Georgian angler carried his gentles to the riverside in a hollow cow horn with cork stoppers at each end. Gentle chutes made from tinned or galvanised metal were made for the Victorian angler while live minnows were carried in bait kettles until well into the twentieth century.

Coarse, sea or game fishermen all landed their fish with a landing net or a gaff. Originally the landing net would have been a home-made item, nothing more

26

No. 165 N
Round Tin Worm or Gentle Box.

No. 165½   Worm Box.

No. 1890
Worm Box.   Double Lid.

No. 5797
Zinc Worm Box.

No. 1468
Gentle Shoot

No. 1104   Gentle Box.

No. 1412
Improved Ground Bait Can.

No 3523   Worm Box

No. 4870   Maggot Box.

No. 3522
Worm Box.

No 5775   Zinc Bait Kettle,
with Sliding Perforated Tray.

No. 6242
Oval May Fly or Gentle Box.

No 166   Tin, Oval,
Bait Kettle

No. 1127   Double Zinc Bait Kettle

No 6172   Floating Zinc Bait Kettle,
with Air Chamber.

No. 166½
Zinc Bait Kettle (Oblong)

No. 6264   Japanned Oval Tin Bait Kettle,
with Removable Perforated Inner Kettle

The full range of live-bait carriers from Allcock's 1912 catalogue.

Left: *An Allcock aluminium cast box embossed with a grayling appeared in their 1912 catalogue.*

Right: *A Hardy bakelite cast box from the 1930s. The screw-threaded top is inlaid with wire decoration in the form of gut casts with flies attached.*

than a willow twig hooped through a net and attached to a long handle. Its only function was to lift a fish clear of the water but it was cumbersome. A long-handled net was acceptable for the static coarse fisherman but for the mobile trout or salmon fisherman a compact folding net was developed.

In 1891 the Hardy catalogue contained details of two examples of folding landing nets. The 'Royde', retailing for £1 3s 6d, had a wooden handle terminating with

Aluminium pocket fly boxes: (top left) with chenille bars; (bottom left) a dry-fly box with lids and leather cast cover; these were both made by Wheatley in the 1930s; (right) a simple fly box with clips made by Hardy Bros about the same time.

Illustrated in the Allcock catalogue of 1866: a tackle book for storing lures, floats and casts, a fly book, two bait needles and a disgorger for removing a hook from a fish.

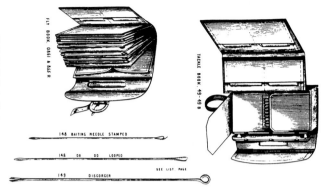

A Georgian live-bait horn for carrying maggots.

A late Victorian tin gentle chute.

A galvanised zinc bait kettle for carrying live minnows.

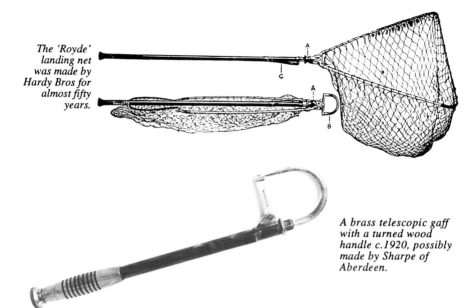

The 'Royde' landing net was made by Hardy Bros for almost fifty years.

A brass telescopic gaff with a turned wood handle c.1920, possibly made by Sharpe of Aberdeen.

Below left: *Long bamboo handles were fitted with a standard screw thread to accept various fittings. Here is a gaff (left), a landing net (bottom) and a wading stick spear (right), while the handle (centre) also held delicate rod tips.*

Below right: *Two Salter spring balances and one Rex balance used by anglers to weigh their catch.*

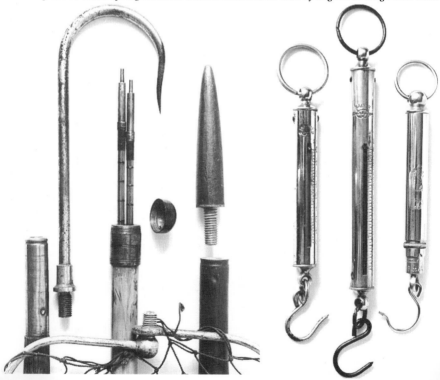

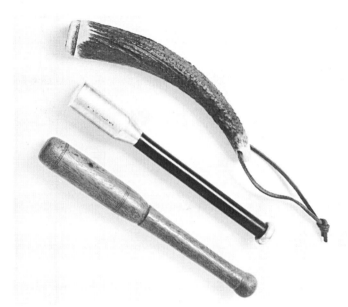

a metal and wire Y-shaped frame which folded and could conveniently be carried on the angler's belt. When the fish was to be landed the net was brought into play with one hand and, by simply throwing the head over the handle, the net opened. One drawback was that it was comparatively short in the handle. H. Cholmondeley-Pennell, a Victorian writer on angling, designed for it a telescopic handle, which could be opened with one action and extended to almost 5 feet (1.5 metres).

Salmon, pike and sea anglers used a gaff, a large, very sharp hook attached to a handle, to lift a fish out of the water when a landing net was not adequate. Boat fishermen used one with a long handle to lift a heavy fish over the side of the boat while salmon or pike fishermen would often carry a short gaff with a telescopic action. The hook of the gaff and the land-ing net were often used on the same handle since the screw thread at the end was standardised for many such items. The bamboo handles were often hollowed out to store delicate cane or wooden rod tips.

River fishermen would carry their fish in a creel. Originally made of leather or wood, the creel is better recognised as the lidded wicker basket which was carried over the angler's shoulder. It could quite easily be submerged in water or lined with damp grass to keep the fish fresh.

The practice of returning fish to the water has long been the convention of coarse fishermen, who have always found their satisfaction in catching, landing and then weighing their quarry. Game fishermen, on the other hand, would keep their salmon and trout. The small cudgel with which the fish were despatched became known as a priest, since it was this which administered the last rites.

FURTHER READING

Benn, Timothy. *The (Almost) Compleat Angler*. Victor Gollancz, 1985.
Buller, Fred, and Falkus, Hugh. *Freshwater Fishing*. Cresset Press, 1975.
Calabi, Silvio. *The Collector's Guide to Antique Fishing Tackle*. Wellfleet Press, USA, 1989.
Graham, Jamie Maxtone. *To Catch a Fisherman*. Published by the author, 1982.
Graham, Jamie Maxtone. *The Best of Hardy's Angler's Guides*. Macdonald, 1989.
Graham, Jamie Maxtone. *Fishing Tackle of Yesterday*. Published by the author, 1989.
Kewley, Charles, and Farrar, Howard. *Fishing Tackle for Collectors*. Elgin Press, 1987.
Sandford, Chris. *The Best of British Baits*. Published by the author, 1998.
Turner, Graham. *Fishing Tackle: A Collector's Guide*. Ward Lock, 1989.
Waller, Philip. *Fishing Reels*. Published by the author, 1993.
Walton, Izaak, and Cotton, Charles. *The Compleat Angler*. First published in 1655; reprinted by various publishers.
Willock, Colin. *The Angler's Encyclopaedia*. Odham's Press, 1960.

PLACES TO VISIT

Intending visitors are advised to find out opening times, and whether items of interest will be on display, before making a special journey.

Forge Mill Needle Museum and Bordesley Abbey Visitor Centre, Forge Mill, Needle Mill Lane, Riverside, Redditch, Worcestershire B98 8HY. Telephone: 01527 62509.
House of Hardy Museum and Countrystore, Willowburn, Alnwick, Northumberland NE66 2PF. Telephone: 01665 510027.